Electric Power

Ed Catherall

Wayland

Young Scientist

Electric Power
Solar Power
Water Power
Wind Power

Hearing
Sight
Taste and Smell
Touch

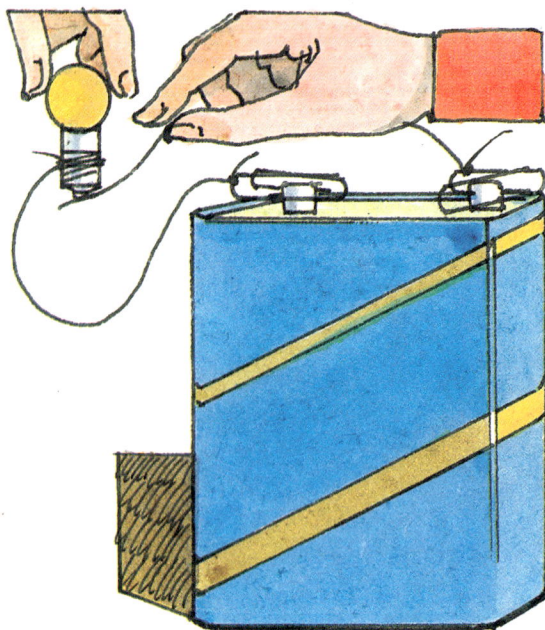

First published in 1981 by Wayland Publishers Limited
49 Lansdowne Place, Hove, East Sussex BN3 1HF, England
© Copyright 1981 Wayland Publishers Limited
ISBN 0 85340 871 8

Illustrated by Ted Draper
Designed and typeset by DP Press Limited, Sevenoaks Kent
Printed in Italy by G. Canale & C.S.p.A, Turin

Contents

Chapter 1 Uses of electric power

Using electricity

You must NEVER play with MAINS electricity. MAINS electricity can KILL. All the experiments in this book use batteries.

Electricity is one of our most convenient sources of power.

Make a list of all your toys which use electricity.
Make a list of all the things that use electricity in your home.
How many different things did you list?

Make a list of all the things that use electricity to give heat.

Make a list of all the things that use electricity to give light.

Make a list of all the things that use electric motors.

Make a list of all the things that use electricity to make magnets.

Which items occur on more than one list?

An electric torch

Switch on an electric torch.
Does it work?

Carefully remove the batteries.
How were the batteries placed in the torch?
What keeps the batteries firmly in place?
What does it say on your batteries?
What size and strength are the batteries?
Do your batteries have positive and negative
signs on them?

Replace your batteries. Does your torch still work?
What happens if you put your batteries back in a
different way?

Making sure that you do not break the glass and
cut yourself, carefully remove the bulb.
What does it say on the bulb? What strength is
the bulb? Is it the same as the battery?
How is the bulb connected to the battery?

Remove the reflector and clean it.

How does the switch work?
Reassemble your torch.
Does it still work?

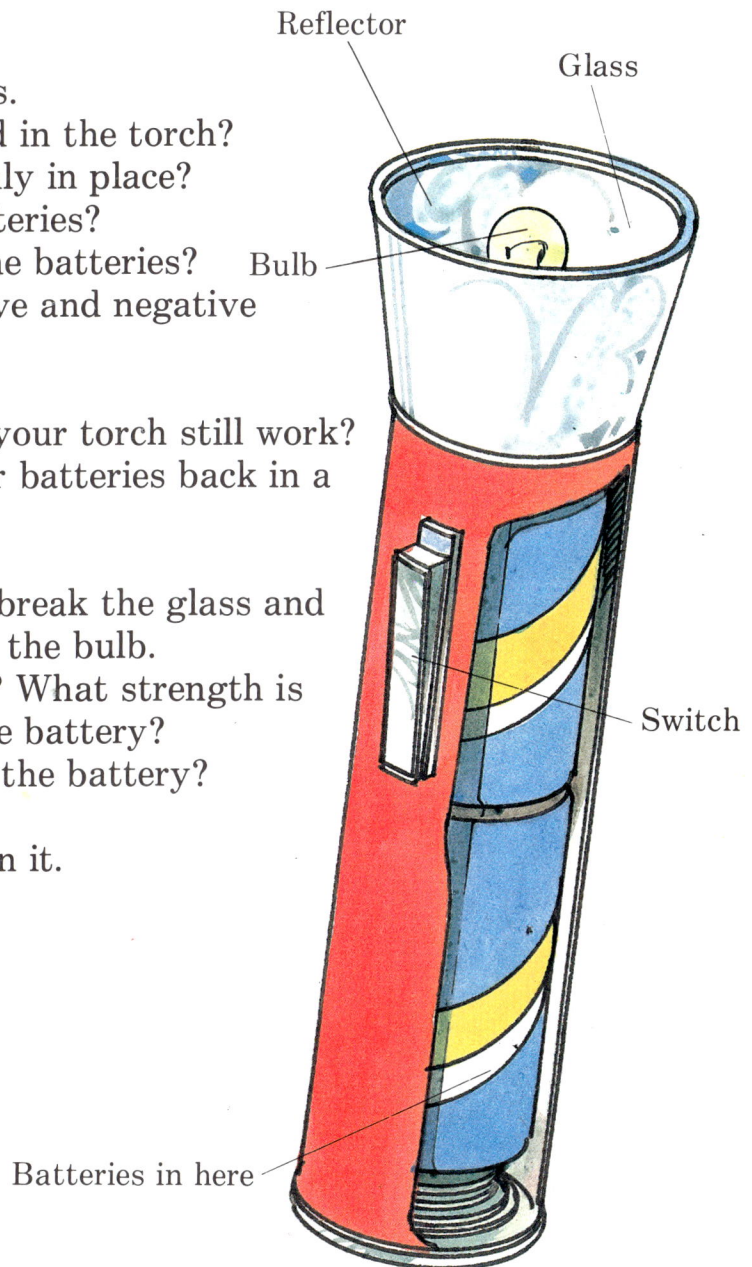

Reflector

Glass

Bulb

Switch

Batteries in here

5

Mending a torch

If your torch does not work, use a fault-finding system. If the torch does not light after you have carried out the first check, try the second check, and so on.

Torch does not light	Torch lights	Fault
1 Check batteries are fitted correctly	→ YES	Wrong connection
2 Change batteries for ones known to work	→ YES	Flat batteries
3 Screw bulb in tightly	→ YES	Poor connection
4 Change bulb for one known to work	→ YES	Bulb broken
5 Examine switch (mend it)	→ YES	Broken switch
6 Examine torch for rust and clean it	→ YES	Poor connections
7 Check all connections and springs	→ YES	Poor connections

Connect a wire to a battery terminal with a paperclip.
Wind the other end of the wire around the stem of a bulb.
Connect another wire to the other battery terminal with a paperclip.
Touch the other end of this wire to the metal centre at the end of the bulb stem.
Does your bulb light?

Make sure that all your connections are clean.
You have made a simple circuit.
Can you invent a holder for the bulb?

Wind here

Touch here

Making a switch

Set up your light circuit as on page 6.
How many ways can you make the light go out?

Find a steel strip from a packing case.
File it to make it clean and smooth.
Use a nail to punch a hole near one end.

Push a round-headed screw
through the hole and start to
screw it into the wood.
Wind a wire around the head of
the screw before you screw it
tightly into the wood.

Underneath the steel strip, fix a
round-headed screw into the
wood.
Wind wire around this screw.

Connect your switch into your
bulb circuit.

When the metal strip is pressed
down, it joins the two wires.
This completes the circuit.
Release the strip and it springs
up, breaking the circuit.

Examine other switches.
How do they work?

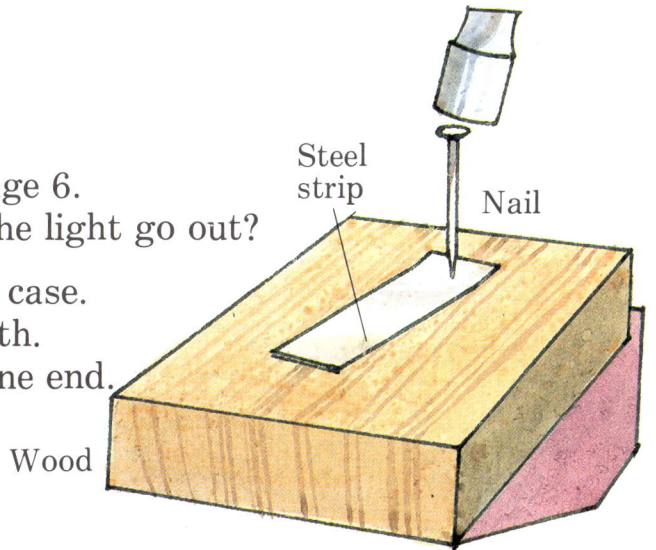

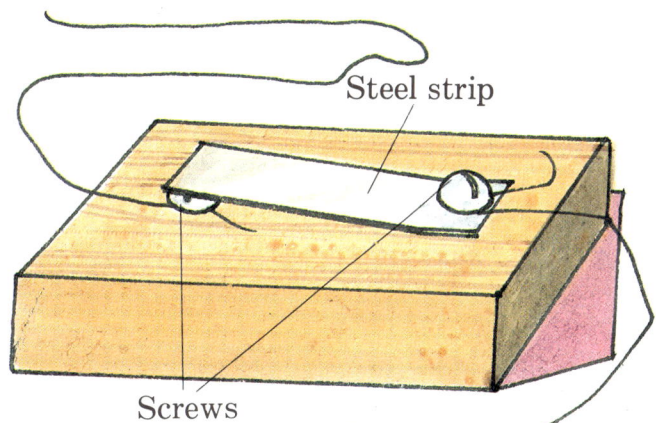

Steel
strip

Nail

Wood

Steel strip

Screws

7

Signalling messages

You can use two light circuits to signal to a friend.
Connect a wire (X) to your bulb.
Connect your bulb to the switch.
Connect two wires (Y and Z) to your switch.
Make another circuit just like this one.

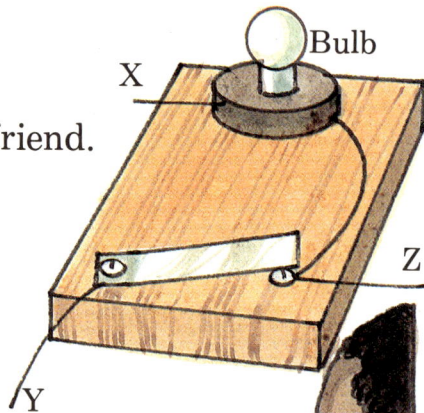

Connect the two circuits together making sure that
the bulb of one is connected to the switch of the other.

Make sure that both bulbs are connected to the battery.
When you press your switch, the bulb on your friend's
side will light up.
Try sending Morse messages.
Morse code uses long flashes (dashes) and short
flashes (dots).

A · -	F · · - ·	K - · -	P · - - ·	U · · -	1 · - - - -	6 - · · · ·
B - · · ·	G - - ·	L · - · ·	Q - - · -	V · · · -	2 · · - - -	7 - - · · ·
C - · - ·	H · · · ·	M - -	R · - ·	W · - -	3 · · · - -	8 - - - · ·
D - · ·	I · ·	N - ·	S · · ·	X - · · -	4 · · · · -	9 - - - - ·
E ·	J · - - -	O - - -	T -	Y - · - -	5 · · · · ·	10 - - - - -
			Z - - · ·			

8

Looking at batteries

Find an old dry cell battery. How can you tell that it is old?

The chemicals inside the battery will damage your clothes, so do not spill the contents.

Cut away the cardboard. The metal case of your battery is made of zinc. Is the zinc discoloured?

Carefully remove the insulation at the top. Lift out the carbon rod. Look inside the battery. The black paste that you see is a mixture of carbon, manganese dioxide and water.
Surrounding the black paste is a white paste, which is a mixture of starch, ammonium chloride and water.
Do not get the paste on your hands.
After investigating your battery, put all the pieces in a plastic bag.
Seal the bag and throw it away.
Wash your hands well.

You can try making your own batteries by using copper and zinc. Place the copper and zinc in strong salt water.
Connect them to a bulb using wire.

Have you made enough electricity to light the bulb?

You might get the bulb to light if you join three batteries together.

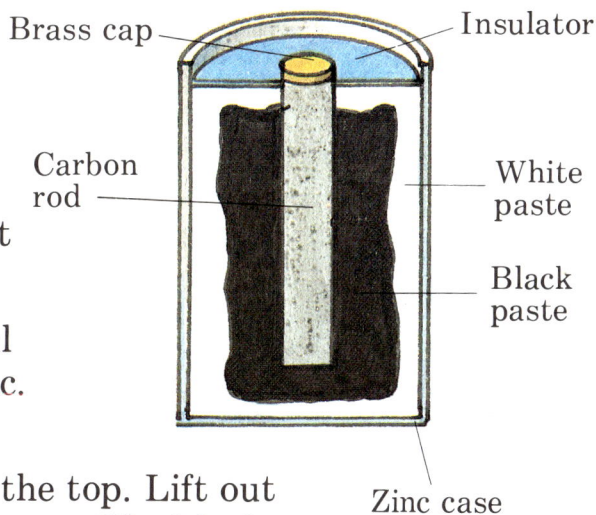

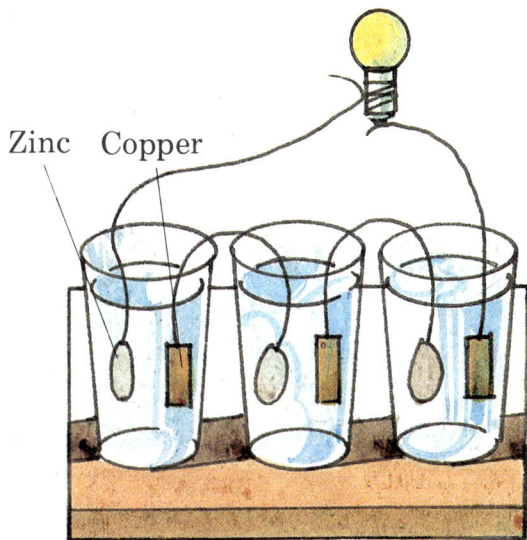

Making a series circuit

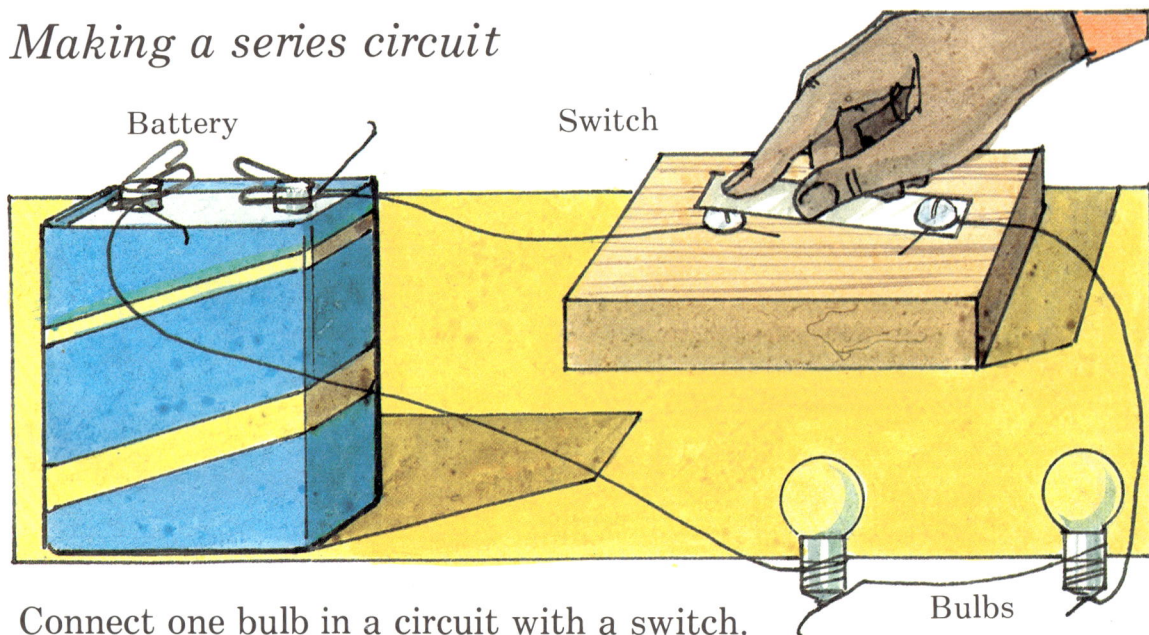

Battery   Switch

Bulbs

Connect one bulb in a circuit with a switch.
Switch on. Does the bulb light up?
Connect two bulbs together.
See that the wire from the centre point of the first
bulb stem winds around the stem of the second bulb.
Switch on. Do both bulbs light up?
Is each bulb as bright as when there was only one in
the circuit?

Connect three bulbs together. What happens?
Unscrew one bulb. Switch on. What happens?
Add another switch to the circuit. What happens?

Set up the circuit with only one bulb in it.
Switch on. See how bright the light is.
Now put another battery in the circuit.
Make sure that the positive of one battery is
connected to the negative of the other.
Switch on. Is the bulb brighter?

Making a parallel circuit

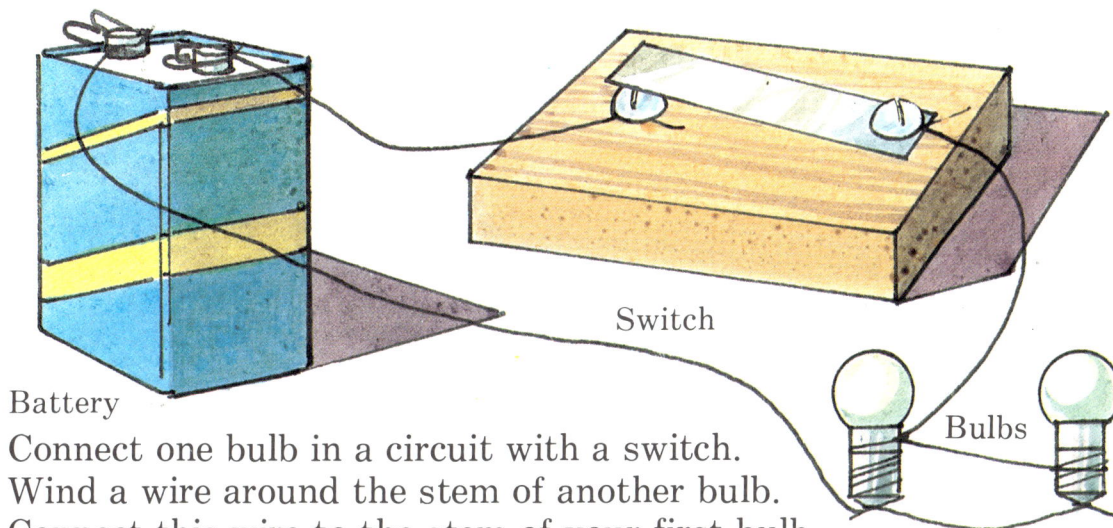

Battery

Switch

Bulbs

Connect one bulb in a circuit with a switch.
Wind a wire around the stem of another bulb.
Connect this wire to the stem of your first bulb.
Connect a wire from the centre of your first bulb to
the centre of your second bulb.
Switch on. Do both bulbs light up?
Is each bulb as bright as when there was only one
bulb in the circuit?

Connect three bulbs together. What happens?

Keep two bulbs in the circuit.
Connect another battery in parallel in the circuit.
To do this, first connect the positive terminals of your
batteries together.
Then connect the negative terminals
of your batteries together.
How bright are the bulbs now?
Disconnect the batteries and reconnect
them in series (see page 10).
How bright are the bulbs?
Is it better for Christmas-tree lights to be
connected in series or parallel? Why?

Making a ring circuit

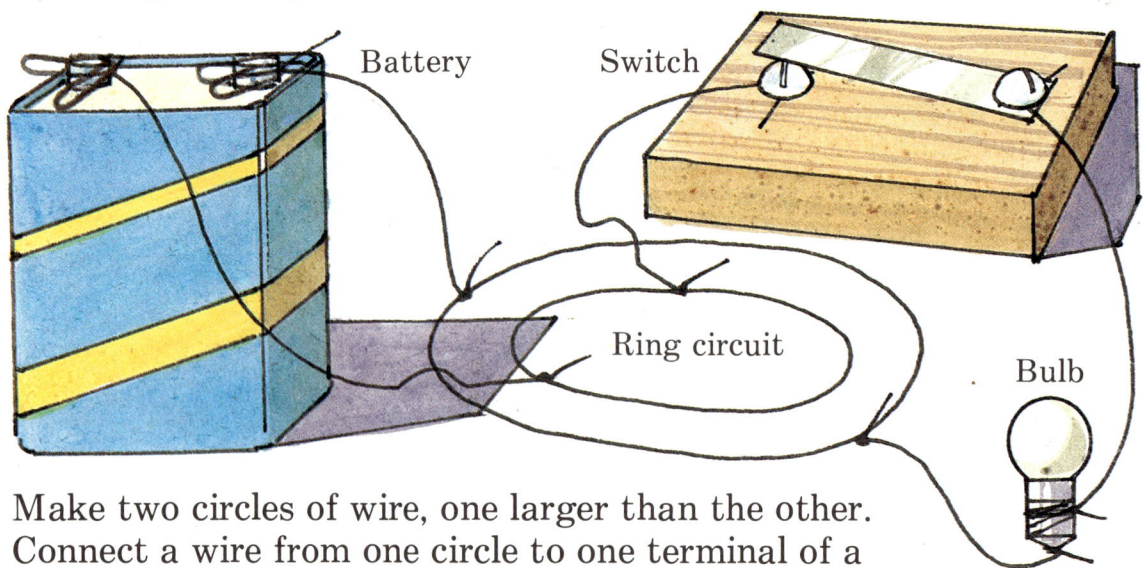

Battery   Switch   Ring circuit   Bulb

Make two circles of wire, one larger than the other.
Connect a wire from one circle to one terminal of a
battery.
Connect another wire from the second circle to the
other terminal of the battery.
If the two circles are not touching, your battery is not
being damaged by shorting it out.

Connect a bulb and a switch together.
Connect one side of the switch to one of the rings.
Connect one side of the bulb to the other ring.
Switch on. Does your bulb light up?
Does it matter where in the ring you connect your
switch and bulb?

Modern houses are wired with a Ring Main Circuit.
Usually, there are at least six parallel rings in a house:
upstairs lighting, upstairs power, immersion heater,
downstairs lighting, downstairs power, and electric
cooker.

Remember, NEVER play with MAINS electricity.

A question and answer board

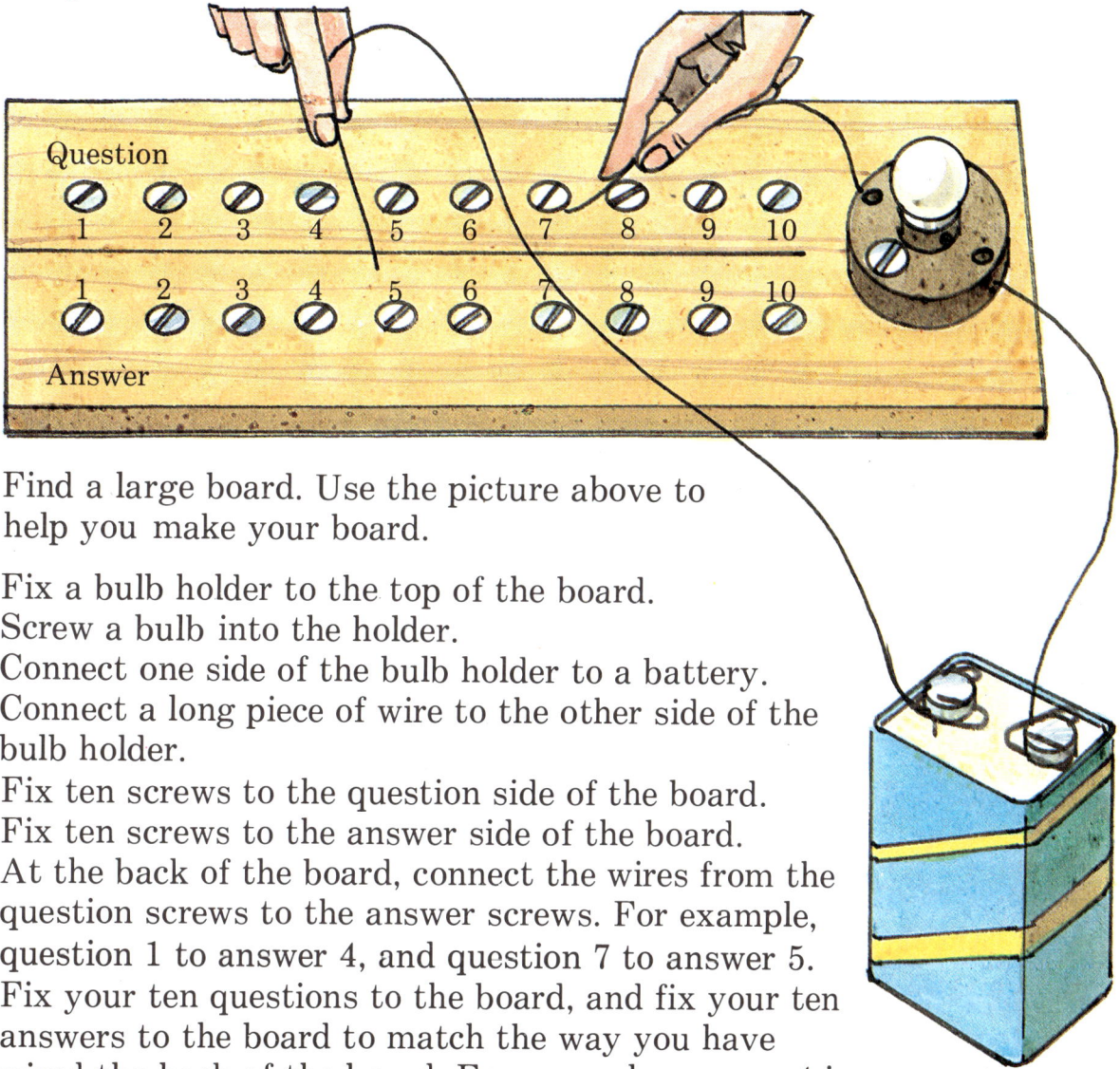

Find a large board. Use the picture above to
help you make your board.

Fix a bulb holder to the top of the board.
Screw a bulb into the holder.
Connect one side of the bulb holder to a battery.
Connect a long piece of wire to the other side of the
bulb holder.
Fix ten screws to the question side of the board.
Fix ten screws to the answer side of the board.
At the back of the board, connect the wires from the
question screws to the answer screws. For example,
question 1 to answer 4, and question 7 to answer 5.
Fix your ten questions to the board, and fix your ten
answers to the board to match the way you have
wired the back of the board. For example, answer 4 is
the correct answer to question 1 and answer 5 to
question 7.
Connect a long wire to the other side of the battery.
Using the two long wires, touch the correct question
and answer to see if your bulb lights up.

Making a conductivity board

Wind a wire around the stem of a bulb.
Connect this wire to a battery.
Connect one end of another wire to the
other battery terminal.
Connect the other end of the wire to
a screw fixed to a wooden board.

Connect a wire from the centre
point of your bulb to another screw
fixed to the wooden board.

Place a metal strip across the two
screws. Does the bulb light up?
Remove the metal strip. What
happens?
The metal strip acts as a switch. It
conducts electricity between the two
screws. Remove the metal strip. What happens?

Put things
to be
tested
across
screws

Try putting a piece of elastic between the two screws.
Does the bulb light?
Does plastic conduct electricity between the two
screws?

Plastic is a non-conductor or an 'insulator'.
Plastic is put around wire to insulate the wire.

How do you know that wood is an insulator?

Try all kinds of materials to see if they are conductors
or insulators.
Record your results.

Sharpen both ends of a pencil.
Is pencil 'lead' a conductor?

14

Variable resistors

Make a collection of different pencils.
Sort them according to hardness.

Soft pencils are almost all graphite.
To make a pencil hard, graphite
is mixed with clay.

Graphite is a form of carbon and
it conducts electricity.

Cut your pencils so that they
are the same length.
Sharpen your pencils at each
end.

Test the conductivity of each
pencil.
What is the relationship of the
brightness of the bulb to the
pencil hardness?

Carefully cut away all the wood
from one side of a pencil.
Connect two wires, one to each
screw of your conductivity board.

Touch each of these wires to
your pencil 'lead'.
Does the bulb light?
Bring the wires closer together.
What happens?

Have you made a dimmer?
Where are dimmers used?

Pencil cut in half

Does water conduct electricity?

Connect two wires, one to each screw of your conductivity board.
Bare the ends of both wires.
Fill a clean jar with distilled water.

Put the two wires in the water.
See that the wires do not touch.
Does your bulb light?
Does water conduct electricity?

Bring the wires close together.
What happens?

Put your hands in the water for a few moments.
Take your hands out and put the wires close together.
What happens?

Stir in some salt.
Does salt water conduct electricity?

Slowly move the wires apart.
What happens?

Look carefully. Can you see any bubbles on your wires?
The electric power is splitting up the water into oxygen and hydrogen gases.

Does tap water conduct electricity?

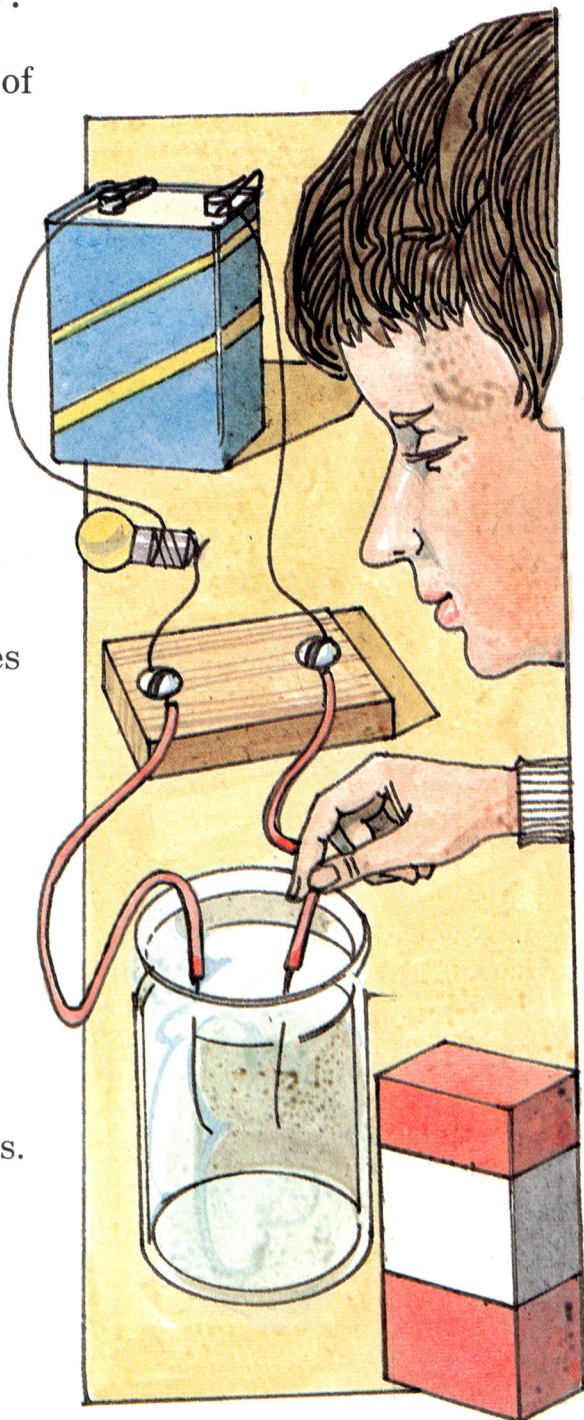

Automatic switches

Find a corked test tube.
Put the bare ends of two wires right
through the cork.
See that the wires do not touch.

Half fill the test tube with salt water.
Connect the two wires from the cork
into a circuit with a bulb.

Does the bulb light?
Turn the tube upside down.
What happens? Why?

Empty out the salt water and fill the
tube with distilled water.

Put a big metal ball bearing in the tube,
and replace the cork with the wires.
Does the bulb light?
Turn the tube upside down.
What happens? Why?

What happens if you replace the water
with cooking oil?
What is the difference?

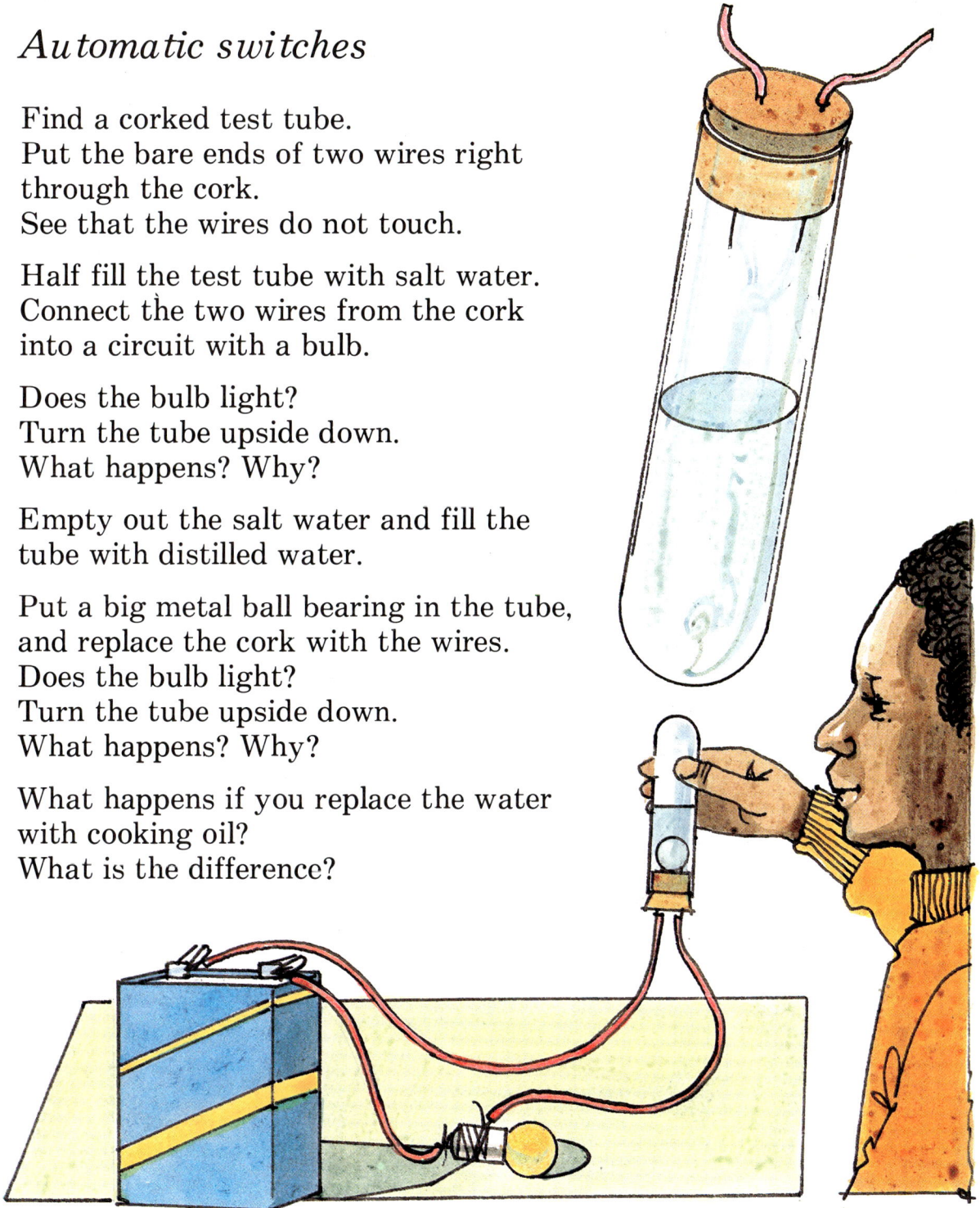

Chapter 3 Electric power works for us

Storing electricity in a lead cell

Make a strong solution of sodium sulphate (Glauber's salt) by dissolving it in water. Half fill a glass or styrofoam cup with your solution.

Cut two lengths of covered bell wire.
Bare both ends of each wire.
Find two strips of lead.
Fix the wires to the lead strips with masking tape.

Drop both lead strips with their connecting wires into your cup of sodium sulphate solution.
You have made an electrical storage cell.

To store electricity in it, connect the other two ends of the wires to a 6-volt battery.
Watch what happens to your storage cell.
Do bubbles appear on your lead strips?
After five minutes, your cell should be charged.

Disconnect the battery.
Connect your storage cell to a torch bulb.
Does your bulb light?
Will it stay lit for five minutes?

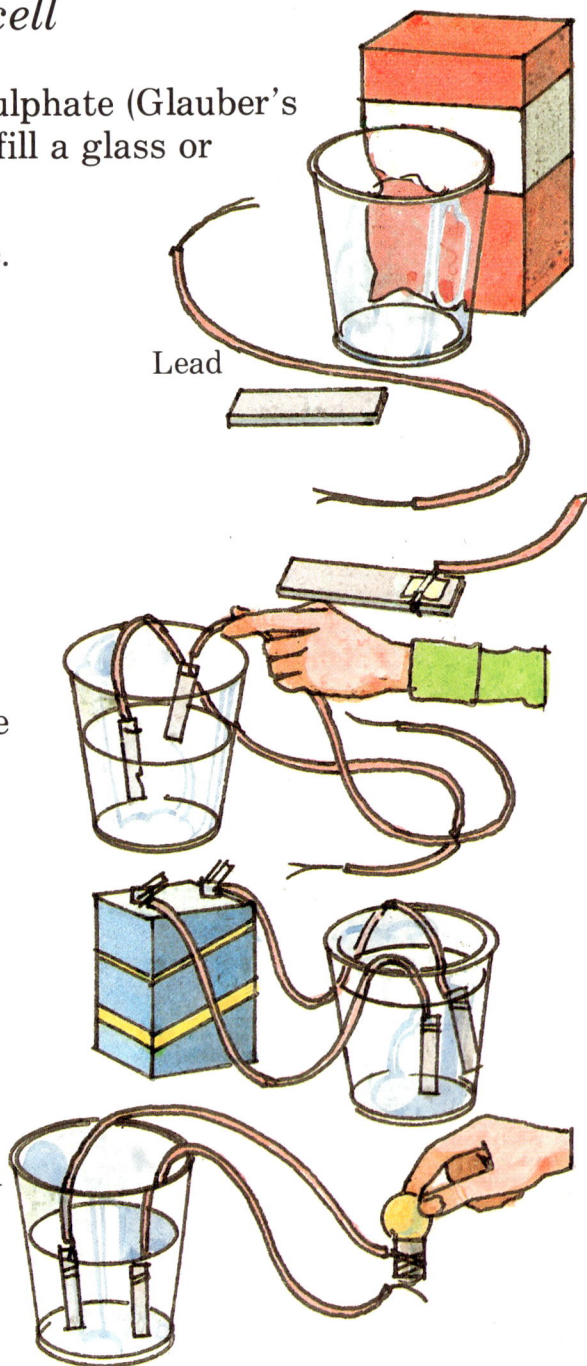

Lead

Heat from electric power

Take a length of covered wire.
Connect the wire to one battery terminal.
Feel the wire. Is it warm?

Connect the wire so that it joins
both battery terminals.
Feel the wire. Is it warm?
Do not leave the wire connected to
the battery for long, or you will ruin
your battery.

Connect together a battery, a
switch and a bulb.
Place the bulb in a glass or styrofoam
cup that is half full of water.
Make sure that only the glass of the
bulb is underwater, not your wire.
Tape the wires to the styrofoam cup
to hold the bulb in place, but do not
switch on yet.
Use a thermometer to test the
temperature of the water.
Wait for the temperature to be
constant. Record the temperature.
Switch on and leave the bulb in
the water for five minutes.
Record the temperature of the
water. How much has the
temperature increased? What
temperature do you get if you heat
the water for ten minutes? What
happens if you use two bulbs?

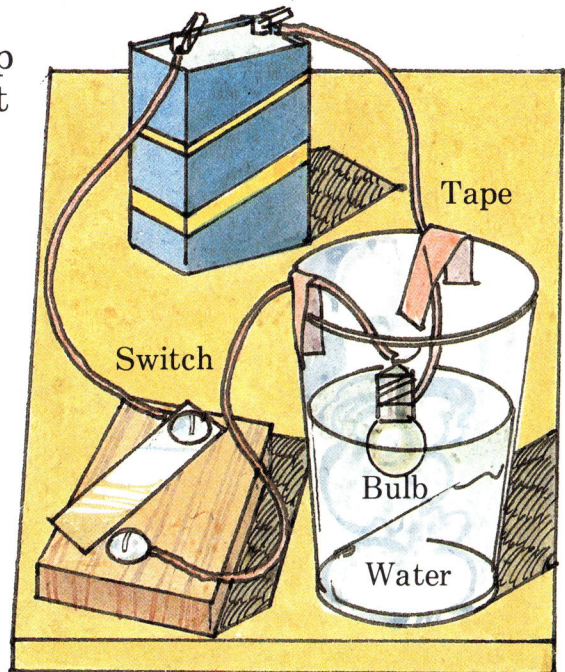

Tape

Switch

Bulb

Water

Electricity and fuses

Look carefully at the filament wire
inside a torch bulb.
How is this filament connected to the
bulb?

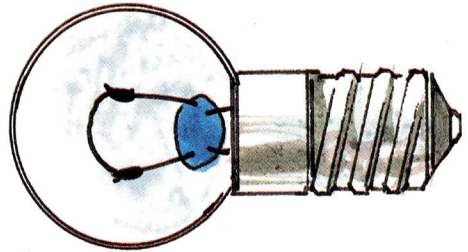

Look at different shapes of bulbs.
Notice how the filaments are connected.

Cut out a bridge shape from very thin
aluminium foil.
Make sure that the centre of your
shape is as small as possible.

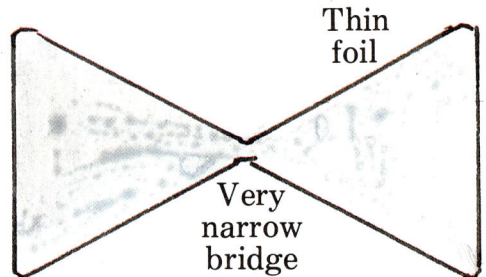

Fix your aluminium shape to a piece of
wood.
Connect one side of your shape to a
battery.
Connect another wire to the other side
of the shape.
With this wire, touch the other battery
terminal.
What happens. Why?

Make another bridge, but this time
make the middle slightly larger.
Repeat the experiment.
What happens?

Look at the nichrome heating wire in
toasters and electric fires.
Do not touch the toaster or fire or you
could be very badly burnt.
Notice how the wires glow and give
heat.

Electroplating

Cut a milk carton in half to make a tank.
Half fill the tank with white vinegar.
Stir salt into the vinegar until no more will dissolve.

Find an old brass key and a piece of copper.
Connect the brass key to the negative terminal
of the battery with wire.
Connect the positive terminal to a switch.
Connect your switch to the piece of copper.

Place the copper and the key in
your tank so that both are just
covered.

Tape the wires to the tank with masking tape.
See that the key and the copper are close
together but not touching.
Switch on. What changes do you notice on the key?
Are bubbles being formed?
If bubbles stick to the key, carefully shake them off.
How long does it take for the key to completely
change colour?
What happens to the copper?

If more batteries are placed in series, will the
key be plated faster?

What happens if you connect the copper to the
negative terminal and the key to the positive
terminal?

Try plating other metals.
Which works best?

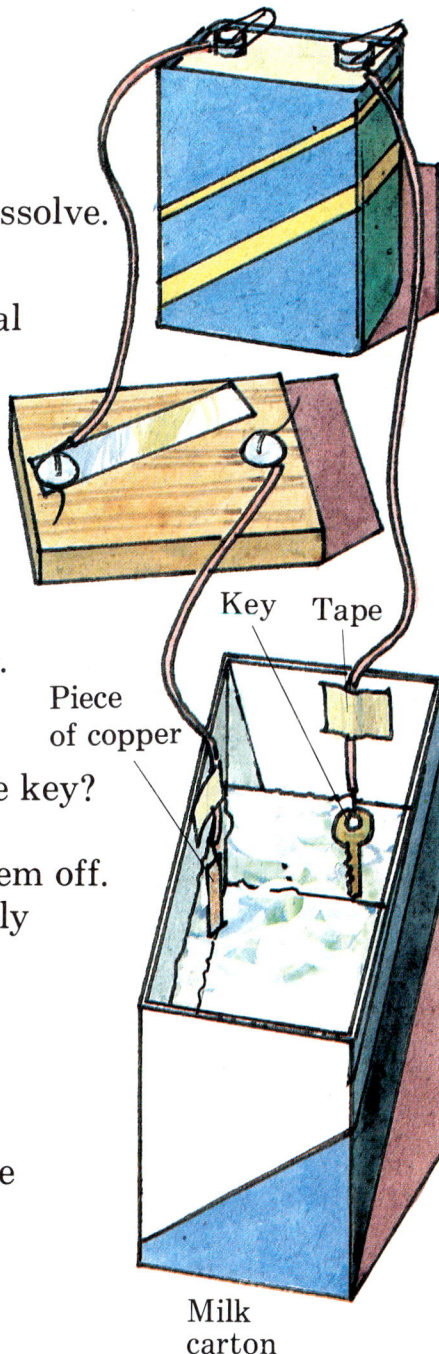

Key   Tape

Piece
of copper

Milk
carton

21

Making an electricity detector

Connect a battery to a switch using covered wire.

Place a compass on the wire.
Which way does your compass point?
See that the wire is in line with the compass needle.

Switch on. What happens to the compass needle when electricity flows along the wire?
Switch off.
What happens? Why?

Place your compass in a small cardboard box such as a matchbox tray.
Repeat the experiment.
Does the box make any difference?

Wind your wire five times around the box.
Switch on.
What happens?
Does the compass needle move more than before?

Wind your wire ten times around the box.
Does this make any difference?

Try using a different battery.
Does the compass needle swing more or less?
Is this battery stronger or weaker?

You have made an 'ammeter'.

What happens if you put a bulb in the circuit?

Switch

Compass

Saving electricity

Look at the electric light bulbs you use at home.

Do you use 40-watt, 60-watt, 75-watt or 100-watt bulbs?

How much brighter is a 100-watt bulb than a 40-watt bulb? Why?

Ten 100-watt bulbs burning in your house for an hour use 1 kilowatt hour.

This meter reads 13672

Your electric meter at home has dials.
Read the dials from left to right and copy down the numbers in the same order.

If the pointer is between numbers, always record the smaller number, since this is the number which the pointer has just passed.

Record how much electricity your house uses in one day.
Record how much electricity your house uses in a week.
How much did this electricity cost?

Think of ways to use less electricity at home.

Chapter 4 Electricity and magnetism

Making an electromagnet

Take a large nail and see if it is magnetized.
Test it by seeing if it will pick up pins.
Wind a length of fine, covered wire around the nail thirty times.
Make sure that you wind the wire the same way.

Connect one end of this wire to a switch and the other end to a battery.

Switch on. Will your nail pick up pins?
How many pins will it pick up? Switch off.

Test another identical nail to see if it is magnetized.

Wind fifty turns of wire around this identical nail.
Switch on. How many pins will this nail pick up?

Is the nail with fifty turns stronger than the one with thirty turns?

Put a compass on a table, and move your nail with thirty turns towards the compass.
How close must this nail be before it affects the compass?

Move your nail with fifty turns towards the compass.
Does this nail affect the compass at a greater distance?

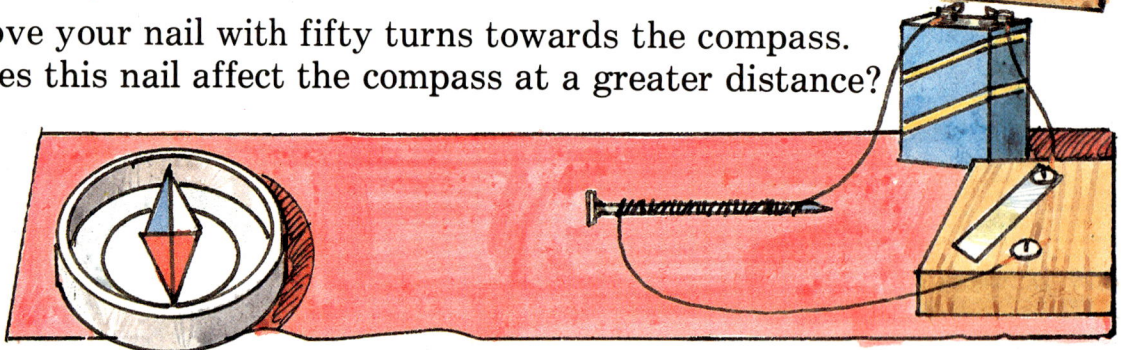

Playing with electromagnets

Make an electromagnet with thirty turns of wire (see page 24).

How near to a compass does your electromagnet have to be before it attracts the compass needle?
Which end of the needle does it attract?
Reverse the battery connections. What happens?

Remove the nail from the coil of wire.
Is your electromagnet stronger or weaker without a nail in the coil?

Wind thirty turns of wire around a wooden rod.
How near to a compass does this electromagnet have to be before it attracts the compass needle?
Which is stronger, the coil with the nail or the coil with the wooden rod?

Wind your coil around many different things.
Which makes the strongest electromagnet?
Use two batteries to power your electromagnet.
Connect them in series (see page 10) and in parallel (see page 11).
Which circuit gives the stronger electromagnet?

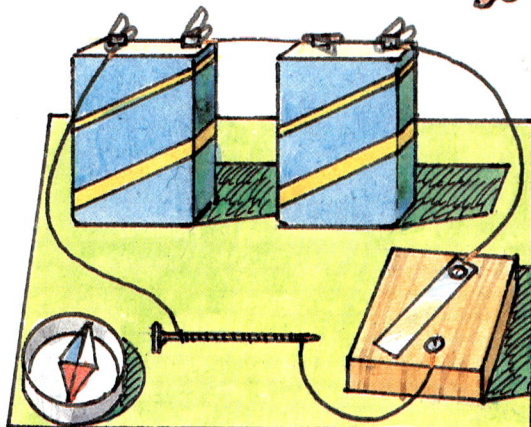

Using electromagnetic power

Make an electromagnet by winding
fifty turns of wire around a nail (see
page 24).

What will your electromagnet pick
up?
Is your electromagnet attracted to
something which is too heavy for it
to pick up?
Make a list of things that your
electromagnet will not pick up.
What are these things made of?
Will your electromagnet pick up all
metal objects? Try a coin.

Will your electromagnet work through wood,
through glass, through water or through a
tin can?
What happens if your electromagnet touches
the tin can?
What happens if you put your electromagnet
inside the tin can, but not actually touching the sides?

Electromagnets are used in telephones.
When you speak into the receiver, the sound pushes
a diaphragm which crushes carbon granules. This
alters the conductivity of the carbon, which alters the
flow of electricity in the wire. This varying flow of
electricity alters the attraction of an electromagnet
and moves another diaphragm so that you can hear
the sounds.

Making a simple electric motor

Find a length of *enamelled* copper wire.
Wind this into a square coil of three turns.
Make sure that the final loops are in the middle
of opposite sides of the square.

Carefully sandpaper away the
top half of the enamel from
both the wires that stick out.

Bend two paperclips into small
loops that will just hold the
enamel-cleared wires.

Fix the two paperclips upright
in balsa wood with two screws.
Make certain that the loops are
wide enough apart to hold the
wire coil.
See that the half-enamelled wires fit inside
the paperclip loops.
Connect a battery and a switch to the two screws.
Place one end of a bar magnet beneath the coil.
Start the coil spinning.
Switch on. What happens?

What happens when you switch off?
What happens if you connect the
battery the other way round?
What happens if you use the
other pole of the magnet?
Does the coil spin faster if it is
made of six turns rather than
three turns?

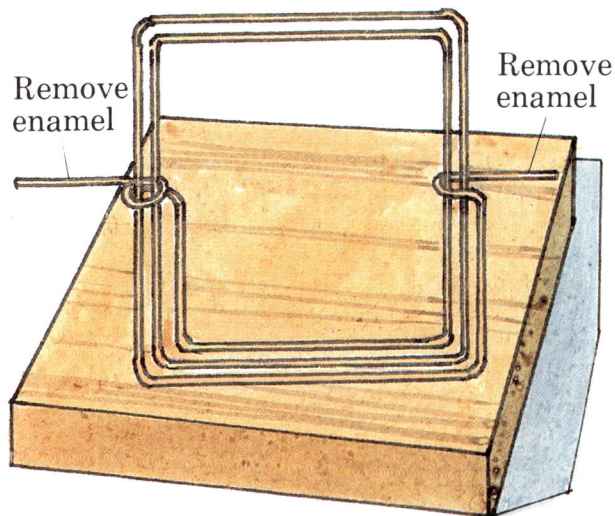

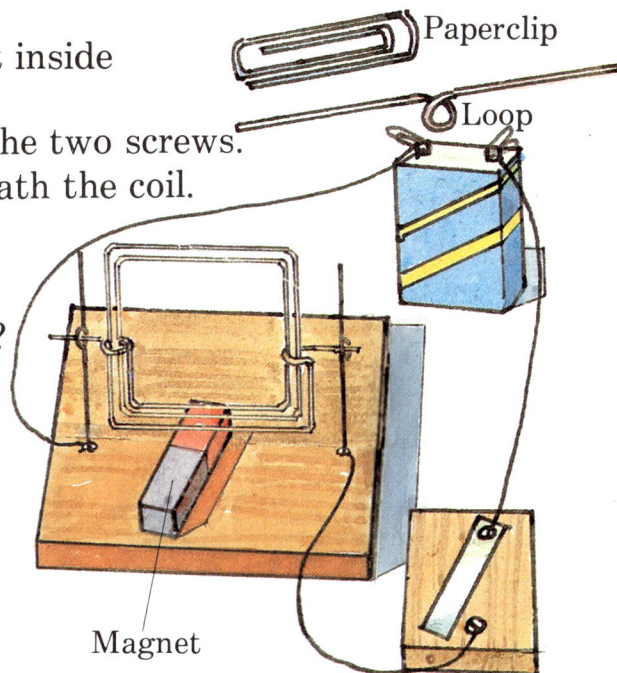

Remove
enamel

Remove
enamel

Paperclip

Loop

Magnet

Making electricity by 'induction'

Take a long length of covered wire.
Wind ten turns of wire around a
compass in a box (see page 22).

Make a large coil at the other
end of the wire.
Make this coil large enough for
a magnet to pass through it,
and join the two ends of the
wire together, as in the picture.
Place a magnet just far enough
away from the compass so that
it does not attract the compass
needle.

Compass
in box

Coil

Move the large coil slowly so that the north pole of
the magnet enters the coil.
Which way does the compass needle move?
Slowly withdraw the magnet. What happens to the
compass needle?

Slowly move the south pole of the magnet
into the coil.
Which way does the compass needle move?

Magnet

If you use a stronger magnet, do you make more
electricity? How can you tell?

What happens if you use two magnets?
How do the magnets have to be placed to make the
most electricity?

What happens if you do this experiment with more
turns of wire in your coil?

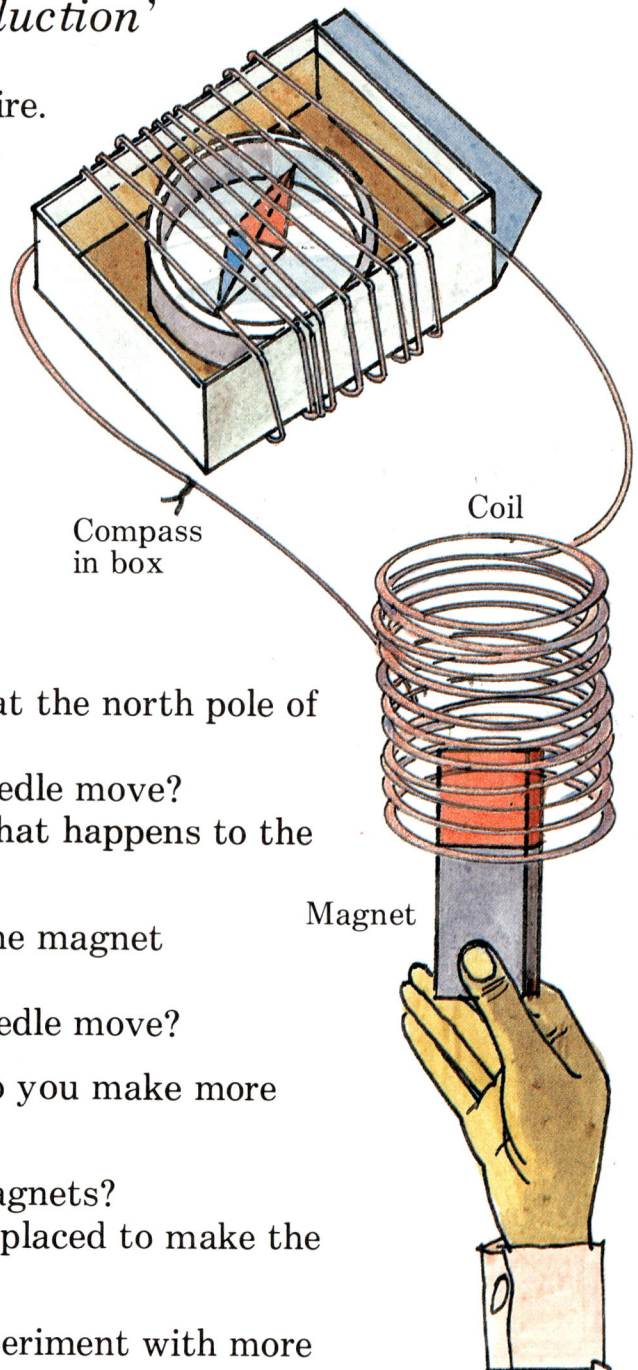

Making a transformer

Make an electromagnet by winding thirty turns of covered wire around one end of a large nail (see page 24). We will call this your first or 'primary' circuit.

Take another length of covered wire. Wind this wire ten times around a compass in a box.
Make a coil of ten turns of wire at the other end.
Join both ends of wire together.

Does the compass needle move?
Is there electricity in this circuit?
We will call this your second or 'secondary' circuit.

Secondary circuit

Place the coil with ten turns of wire from your secondary circuit onto your electromagnet nail.
Switch on. Does the compass needle move?
Is there electricity in your secondary circuit?
If the two circuits are not connected, how does electricity form in the second circuit?

What happens if you have twenty turns of wire around the electromagnet nail in your primary circuit, and thirty turns of wire in the coil of your secondary circuit.

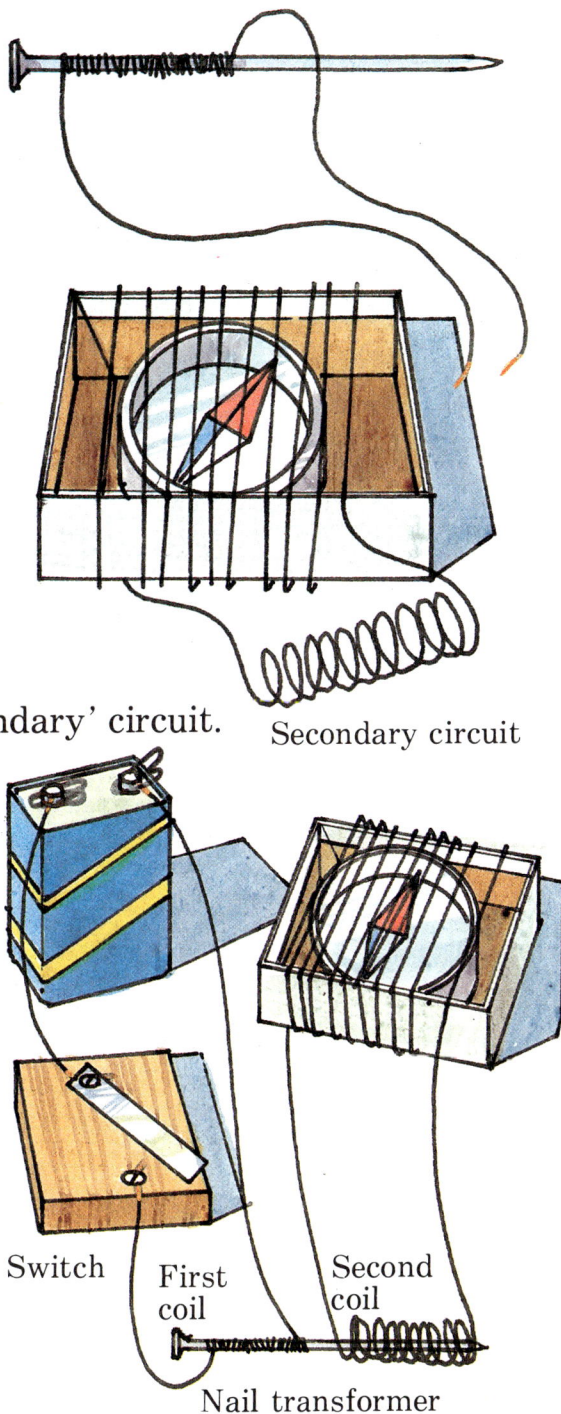

Switch   First coil   Second coil

Nail transformer

29

Static electricity

Tear newspaper into small pieces.
Hold a plastic comb near the paper pieces.
What happens?
Comb your clean, dry hair.
Hold the plastic comb near the paper pieces.
What happens?

Look into a mirror and comb your hair
until it is charged with static electricity.

Hold your comb close to your hair.
What happens?

Rub your comb with wool.
Is your comb charged with static electricity?
Where does wool come from?
Is the wool charged with static electricity?
How can you find out?

Rub a plastic pen with wool.
Is the pen charged?
Is the charge strongest at the ends?
Will the middle of the pen pick up pieces of paper?
Will a charged pen pick up pieces of metal foil?

Try rubbing your pen with other
materials.
Do these materials charge your
pen with static electricity?

Try rubbing other things with wool. Do
these other things become charged?

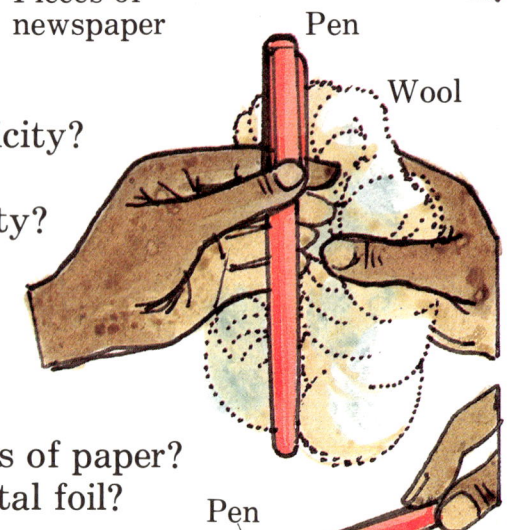

Comb

Pieces of
newspaper

Pen

Wool

Pen

Metal foil

30

What will static electricity do?

Turn on a water tap so that the water comes out in a thin stream.
Charge a plastic pen (see page 30) and hold it close to the water stream.
What happens?

Turn the water tap until the water comes out as a stream of drops.

Hold a charged pen near the drops.
What happens?

Have you seen large raindrops during a thunderstorm?

Blow up a balloon and tie the neck.
Rub the balloon carefully with wool.
Will the charged balloon pick up pieces of paper?
Will the charged balloon stick to the wall?

Hold a hair from your head close to a charged balloon.
What happens?

Drop some chalk dust onto a charged balloon.
What happens to the dust?
What do you notice about the charge on the balloon?

Rub a balloon on one side only with wool.
Put the balloon on a table with the charged side facing upward.
What happens?

Charged pen

Water drops

One hair

Balloon

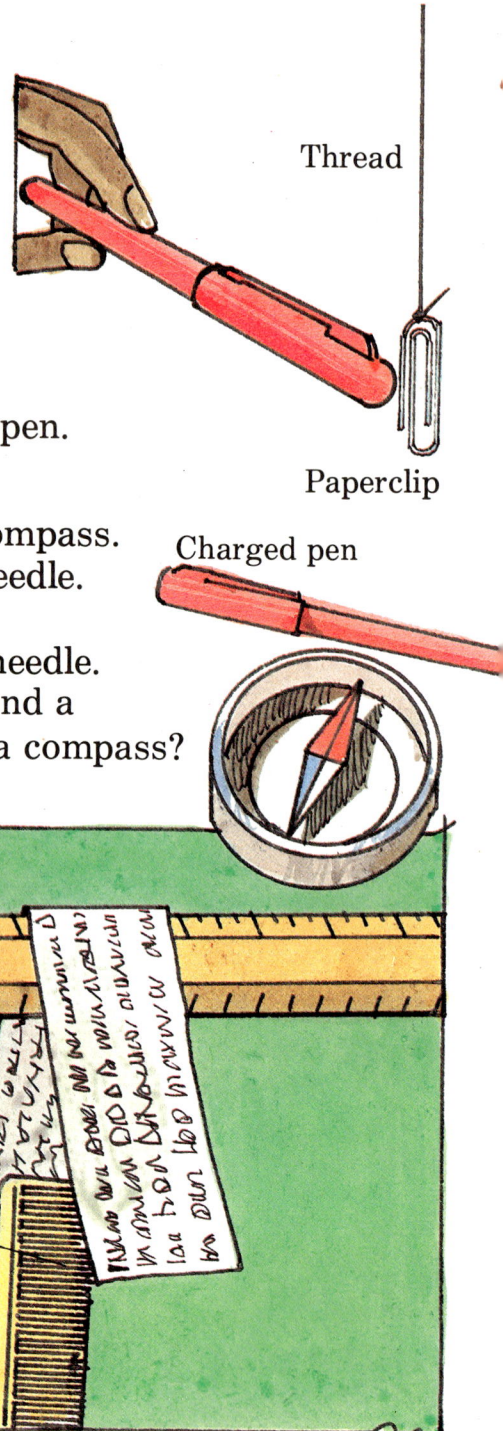

Detecting static charges

Hang a paperclip from a silk thread.
Hold a charged pen close to the paperclip.
Is the paperclip attracted?

Rub your finger along the charged pen.
Is the paperclip attracted now?

Unravel one end of a silk thread.
Hold the unravelled end close to a charged pen.
What happens?

Remove the glass cover from a magnetic compass.
Hold a charged pen close to the compass needle.
What happens?
Hold the pen close to the other end of the needle.
Is there any difference between a magnet and a
charged pen when they are placed close to a compass?
Replace the glass cover.
Repeat the experiment.
What happens?

Cut a long, thin strip of newspaper.
Fold it in half. Open the fold and
put it on a table.
Stroke the paper with wool.
Pick up the paper with a ruler so
that both halves hang down.
What happens to the paper?
Rub your finger along the paper.
What happens?
Charge a plastic comb and hold it
between the halves of the paper strip.
What happens?

Thread

Paperclip

Charged pen

Wooden ruler

Charged comb